6 – 16

D1060800

# HOCKEY TRIVIA

## By Dan Myers

SportsZone
An Imprint of Abdo Publishing
abdopublishing.com

**abdopublishing.com**

Published by Abdo Publishing, a division of ABDO, PO Box 398166, Minneapolis, Minnesota 55439. Copyright © 2016 by Abdo Consulting Group, Inc. International copyrights reserved in all countries. No part of this book may be reproduced in any form without written permission from the publisher. SportsZone™ is a trademark and logo of Abdo Publishing.

Printed in the United States of America, North Mankato, Minnesota
082015
012016

Cover Photo: Carlos Osario/AP Images
Interior Photos: Carlos Osario/AP Images, 1, 4–5; AP Images, 7, 21; Bill Janscha/AP Images, 9; Dennis Floss/AP Images, 11; Chris Carlson/AP Images, 12; Gene J. Puskar/AP Images, 14; Fred Jewell/AP Images, 17; Tom Pidgeon/AP Images, 19; Christopher Szagola/Cal Sport Media/AP Images, 22; Mike Blake/Reuters/Newscom, 25; Itsuo Inouye/AP Images, 27; Chris O'Meara/AP Images, 29; Anthony Nesmith/Cal Sport Media/AP Images, 31; Paul Sancya/AP Images, 32; Kevin Frayer/AP Images, 35, 37; LM Otero/AP Images, 39; Kevork Djansezian/AP Images, 41; Brian Kersey/AP Images, 42

Editor: Patrick Donnelly
Series Designer: Jake Nordby

**Library of Congress Control Number: 2015945766**

**Cataloging-in-Publication Data**
Myers, Dan.
 Hockey trivia / Dan Myers.
   p. cm. -- (Sports trivia)
 ISBN 978-1-68078-004-8 (lib. bdg.)
 Includes bibliographical references and index.
 1. Hockey--Miscellanea--Juvenile literature.   2. Sports--Miscellanea--Juvenile literature.   I. Title.
 796.962--dc23

                                                        2015945766

# CONTENTs

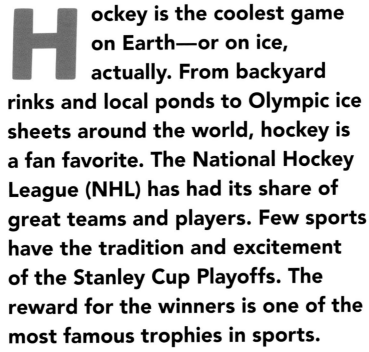

**H**ockey is the coolest game on Earth—or on ice, actually. From backyard rinks and local ponds to Olympic ice sheets around the world, hockey is a fan favorite. The National Hockey League (NHL) has had its share of great teams and players. Few sports have the tradition and excitement of the Stanley Cup Playoffs. The reward for the winners is one of the most famous trophies in sports.

How well do you know hockey? Read on and test your knowledge!

*All statistics and answers are current through the 2014–15 NHL season.

# CHAPTER 1

# ROOKIE

**Q** What is the name of the trophy awarded to the champion of the NHL?

**A** The Stanley Cup was purchased by Sir Frederick Arthur Stanley, a Canadian politician. Stanley donated the cup in 1892. It was to be presented to "the championship hockey club of the Dominion of Canada." The National Hockey Association of Canada gained possession of the Cup in 1910. That league stopped playing in 1917. For the next decade, the winners of the Western or Pacific Coast leagues would play the champion of the NHL in the Stanley Cup Finals. After that, the NHL became the sole owner of the Cup.

Members of the New York Rangers gather around the Stanley Cup in 1940.

**Q** Which NHL clubs are known as "the Original Six"?

**A** The NHL was a six-team league from 1942–43 until 1966–67. Those six teams were not the first six NHL teams. But fans remember them as "the Original Six." Two of the teams were in Canada—the Montreal Canadiens and the Toronto Maple Leafs. The other four were the Boston Bruins, the Chicago Blackhawks, the Detroit Red Wings, and the New York Rangers. All six remain high-profile clubs in today's NHL.

**Q** How many of the NHL's 30 teams are located in Canadian cities?

**A** Canada is home to seven NHL teams. The Montreal Canadiens and the Toronto Maple Leafs are the oldest. They have been in the league since 1917. The other five are the Calgary Flames, the Edmonton Oilers, the Ottawa Senators, the Vancouver Canucks, and the Winnipeg Jets.

**Q** Which coach has the most wins in NHL history?

**A** Scotty Bowman won 1,244 games in 30 seasons behind the bench. He coached five teams and won the Stanley Cup nine times. Longtime New York Islanders coach Al Arbour is in second place with 782 victories.

**Q** Which hockey legend was nicknamed "the Great One"?

**A** Wayne Gretzky scored a record 2,857 points in 20 NHL seasons. He led the Edmonton Oilers to four Stanley Cup championships in his nine seasons there. Later he helped hockey grow in popularity in

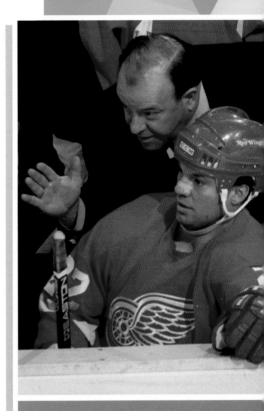

Scotty Bowman offers advice to Dino Ciccarelli on the Detroit Red Wings bench.

the United States when he played for the Los Angeles Kings. The NHL retired Gretzky's No. 99 throughout the league when he retired after the 1998–99 season.

Q Which team has won the most Stanley Cups?

A The Montreal Canadiens have won the Stanley Cup 24 times. Their first championship came in 1916. Included in those 24 championships is a record run of five consecutive titles between 1956 and 1960. They also won four straight championships between 1976 and 1979. The Toronto Maple Leafs are second with 13 titles. The Detroit Red Wings are next with 11.

Q Who scored the most goals in a single season?

A Wayne Gretzky scored 92 goals in 80 games during the 1981–82 season. He shattered the previous record of 76, set by Boston's Phil Esposito in 1970–71. Gretzky threatened his own record two years later when he scored 87 goals. That is the second-highest total in a season.

Phil Esposito, *right*, congratulates Wayne Gretzky after Gretzky broke Esposito's single-season goal-scoring record.

**A** Teemu Selanne debuted with the Winnipeg Jets in 1992. He quickly made a name for himself. Selanne scored 76 goals and had 132 points as a rookie. Selanne was traded to the Mighty Ducks of Anaheim in 1996. He played 15 seasons over two stints with the Ducks. He finished his career with 684 goals and 1,457 points.

**Q** What is a hockey puck made of?

**A** Pucks are made of rubber that has been vulcanized. That means the natural rubber has been converted into a stronger material. Players can shoot pucks at speeds approaching 100 miles per hour (161 km/h). A puck must be sturdy to survive that kind of force. NHL pucks weigh six ounces (170 g). They are three inches (7.6 cm) across and one inch (2.5 cm) thick. They are also frozen before they are used in a game. That keeps them from bouncing on the ice.

**Q** What is it called when a player scores three goals in a game?

**A** That is a hat trick. The term is believed to date back to the 1940s. A store owner in Toronto gave free hats to Maple Leafs players who scored three goals in a game. Today some fans throw their hats onto the ice after a player's third goal in a game. Scoring three goals in a row is a natural hat trick.

WHO DID THE PITTSBURGH PENGUINS SELECT WITH THE FIRST PICK OF THE 2005 NHL DRAFT?

The Penguins drafted Sidney Crosby first overall that year. Crosby scored 39 goals and had 102 points as a rookie during the 2005–06 season. He finished second in voting for the Calder Trophy. That is awarded to the NHL's top rookie each year.

# CHAPTER 2

## VETERAN

**Q** Which Hall of Fame defenseman played for 22 years before winning his first Stanley Cup in his final NHL season in 2001?

**A** Ray Bourque is considered one of the best players in NHL history. He was a five-time winner of the Norris Trophy, which is given to the league's best defenseman. But in 20 seasons with the Boston Bruins, he never won a Stanley Cup. The Bruins traded him to the Colorado Avalanche in 2000. The next year the Avalanche defeated the New Jersey Devils in seven games in the Stanley Cup Finals. Bourque finally had his championship.

Ray Bourque finally hoists the Stanley Cup after winning it with the Avalanche.

**Q** Which NHL team is the oldest?

**A** The Montreal Canadiens are older than the NHL itself. The Canadiens started play in 1909. The league was founded in 1917.

**Q** Where is the Hockey Hall of Fame located?

**A** The Hockey Hall of Fame is in Toronto, Canada. It opened in 1961. The US Hockey Hall of Fame opened in 1973 in Eveleth, Minnesota.

**Q** Which team holds the record for most wins in a season?

**A** The 1995–96 Detroit Red Wings won 62 games. They finished the season with 62 wins, 13 losses, and 7 ties. The 1976–77 Canadiens won 60 games. However, they played two fewer games than the 1995–96 Red Wings.

**Q** Which team scored the most goals in an NHL game?

**A** The Montreal Canadiens beat the Quebec Bulldogs 16–3 on March 3, 1920. The Canadiens are also a part of the

record for combined goals in a single game. They had set that record just weeks earlier when they defeated the Toronto St. Patricks 14–7.

**Q** Who is the only person to have played in five decades as an NHL player?

**A** Gordie Howe started with the Detroit Red Wings in 1946. He was just 18 years old. Howe played 25 seasons in Detroit and retired in 1971. After sitting out for two seasons, Howe came back. He played in the World Hockey Association (WHA) for six seasons. When the WHA folded, a few teams—including Howe's New England Whalers—joined the NHL. During the 1979–80 season, Howe played in 80 games for the Hartford Whalers. He scored 15 goals and had 26 assists—at age 51. He retired a few weeks after he turned 52.

**Q** Which team has retired the most numbers?

**A** The Montreal Canadiens have retired 15 numbers. That total actually honors 18 different players. The numbers 5, 12, and 16 each represent two players.

**Q** Who was the first player to sign a $1 million contract?

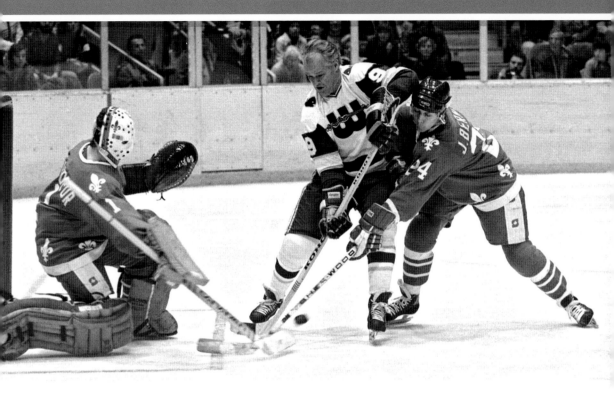

A The Winnipeg Jets paid Bobby Hull $1 million to jump from the NHL to the WHA in 1972. Hull had been a star with the Chicago Blackhawks for 15 years. The WHA needed a few big names to leave the NHL and join the new league. The Jets' owners offered him $2.5 million over 10 years, with $1 million paid up front. He agreed and the WHA had its first big star. It did not hurt that Hull's nickname was "the Golden Jet."

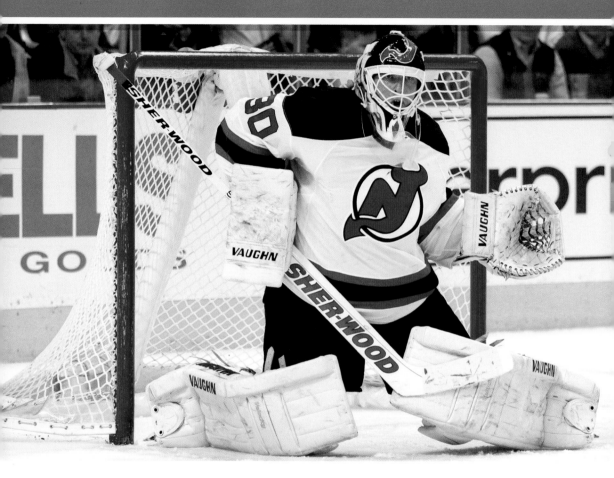

Martin Brodeur was a longtime star in the nets for the New Jersey Devils.

## Q Which two NHL teams are the newest?

A The Minnesota Wild and the Columbus Blue Jackets each began play during the 2000–01 season. The Winnipeg Jets have only been around since 2011. But that team had previously played as the Atlanta Thrashers.

**Who was the first NHL player to score 50 goals in a season?**

**A** Maurice "The Rocket" Richard scored 50 goals during the 1944–45 season. Each NHL team played only 50 regular-season games from 1942–43 to 1945–46. So Richard averaged a goal per game. The Canadiens' sharpshooter was the only player to do it for 16 years. The next player to score 50 goals in a season was Montreal's Bernie Geoffrion in 1960–61. By then the regular season was 70 games long.

## WHICH GOALTENDER HOLDS THE NHL RECORD FOR CAREER VICTORIES?

Martin Brodeur had 691 career wins. All but three of them came with the New Jersey Devils. Brodeur played in New Jersey from 1992–2014. He joined the St. Louis Blues early in the 2014–15 season. Brodeur won three more games there before retiring. Brodeur also played in a record 1,266 games. He won 140 more games than Patrick Roy, who has the second-most career victories.

# CHAPTER 3

# CHAMPION

**Q** Which two teams participated in the first outdoor game in NHL history?

**A** The Montreal Canadiens faced the Edmonton Oilers on November 22, 2003. The Heritage Classic was a big success. The game at Commonwealth Stadium—home of the Canadian Football League's Edmonton Eskimos—drew more than 57,000 fans. It also had the second-highest television ratings for a regular-season game in history. The NHL took the concept across the border on January 1, 2008. The Buffalo Sabres hosted the Pittsburgh Penguins in the first annual Winter Classic.

**Steam pours off Canadiens goalie Jose Theodore during the Heritage Classic.**

**Who is the first goaltender to score a goal in an NHL game?**

A Billy Smith of the New York Islanders made history on November 28, 1979. The Colorado Rockies had pulled their goalie for an extra attacker. A Rockies pass was off target. It skidded the length of the ice and into the empty net. Smith was the last Islander to touch the puck, so he got credit for the goal. Since then, 10 other goaltenders have scored in a game.

Q **Which two teams took part in the first NHL regular-season game played outside of North America?**

A The Vancouver Canucks and the Mighty Ducks of Anaheim played a game in Japan on October 3, 1997. Japan was set to host the Winter Olympics in February 1998. NHL players were preparing to play in the Olympics for the first time. Hockey is not a popular sport in Japan. So the NHL wanted to help its citizens become more familiar with it. The Canucks and the Ducks played

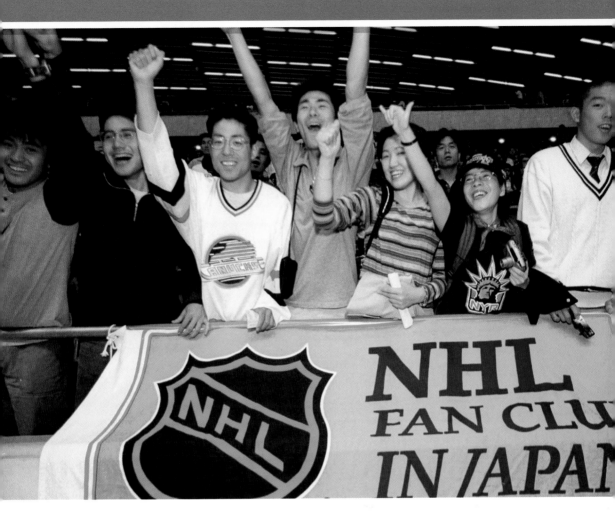

**Japanese fans embraced the NHL when it arrived in 1997.**

two games in two days at Tokyo's Yoyogi Arena. The teams split a pair of 3–2 games.

**Q Who holds the NHL record for career penalty minutes?**

**A** Dave "Tiger" Williams spent more time in the penalty box than any other player in NHL history. Williams played for five teams between 1974 and 1988. In that time, he racked up 3,966 penalty minutes. He topped 300 penalty minutes in a season six times. Williams did much more than take penalties, though. He also scored 241 goals and had 513 points in 962 career games.

**Q  Who was the first woman to play in an NHL game?**

**A** Manon Rheaume played goalie for the Tampa Bay Lightning. Her appearance came in a preseason game against the St. Louis Blues on September 23, 1992. Rheaume gave up two goals in one period. She played in another preseason game for the Lightning the next year. Rheaume went on to spend parts of five seasons playing in the men's minor leagues. She also was the goalie for the Canadian women's national team. Rheaume won two world championships and an Olympic silver medal with Team Canada.

Manon Rheaume listens to the national anthem before playing for the Tampa Bay Lightning on September 23, 1992.

**Q** Who are the only two coaches to win the Stanley Cup with more than one team?

**A** Tommy Gorman won the Cup in back-to-back years. He led the Chicago Blackhawks to the title in 1934. The next year he won the Cup with the Montreal Maroons.

Scotty Bowman won the Stanley Cup with three different teams. He won five with the Montreal Canadiens between 1973 and 1979. He won another one with the Pittsburgh Penguins in 1992. Bowman then led the Detroit Red Wings to the title in 1997, 1998, and 2002.

**Q Which goaltender has the highest career save percentage?**

**A** Finnish star Tuukka Rask of the Boston Bruins has stopped 92.6 percent of the shots he has faced. Rask won the Vezina Trophy as the NHL's best goaltender after the 2013–14 season. He was a backup when the Bruins won the Stanley Cup in 2011.

**Q Who was the first NHL goaltender to wear a mask?**

**A** Most people think the answer is Jacques Plante of the Montreal Canadiens. He made the goalie mask a familiar piece of gear when he started wearing one in 1959. But the first goaltender to wear a mask in an NHL game was actually Clint Benedict of the Montreal Maroons.

Benedict spent 13 years in the NHL. He first put on a mask in 1930, his final year in the league. But Benedict played only five more NHL games after that. Nobody else wore a mask until Plante did it 29 years later.

**Q** When did the NHL adopt a five-minute sudden-death overtime period for regular-season games?

**A** Sudden-death overtime was reintroduced for regular-season play in the 1983–84 season. The league has used overtime in some form ever since. The NHL had stopped using sudden-death overtime in 1942 due to wartime restrictions on train travel. The United States and Canada were fighting in World War II at the time. Overtime did not return for more than 40 years.

**Q** **Who holds the single-season goals-per-game record in NHL history?**

**A** Joe Malone of the Montreal Canadiens scored 44 goals in 20 games during the 1917–18 season. At 2.20 goals per game, he is the only player in NHL history to average more than two goals per game.

## WHO HOLDS THE ALL-TIME RECORD FOR MOST GAMES PLAYED IN THE STANLEY CUP PLAYOFFS?

Defenseman Chris Chelios played in 266 career playoff games. He also is fifth all-time with 1,651 regular-season games played. Chelios spent most of his career with Montreal, Chicago, and Detroit. He retired after playing seven games with the Atlanta Thrashers in 2010—at age 48!

# CHAPTER 4

# HALL OF FAMER

**Q** Which pair of brothers holds the NHL record for combined goals in a single season?

**A** During the 1999–2000 season, Pavel Bure of the Florida Panthers led the NHL with 58 goals. His brother, Valeri Bure of the Calgary Flames, scored 35. Their total of 93 goals was a record for brothers. Bobby and Dennis Hull are second, with a combined 88 goals for the Chicago Blackhawks during the 1968–69 season.

**Q** Who was the first commissioner of the NHL?

**A** Gary Bettman was named the commissioner of the NHL on February 1, 1993. He is the only person ever to have

The Bure brothers—Pavel, *left*, and Valeri—
celebrate a goal in the 2000 All-Star Game.

held the office. Before 1993 the NHL president was the highest-ranking official in the league.

**Q** **Which team has the longest streak of consecutive appearances in the Stanley Cup Playoffs?**

**A** The Boston Bruins reached the playoffs in 29 straight seasons between 1968 and 1996. During the span, the Bruins won the Stanley Cup twice. They finished as the runners-up five times.

**Q** **What are the names of the NHL's two Most Valuable Player trophies?**

**A** The Hart Memorial Trophy is awarded to "the player deemed most valuable to his team." Members of the Professional Hockey Writers Association vote to decide the winner. The Ted Lindsay Award goes to the league's "most outstanding player." Members of the NHL Players Association (NHLPA) vote to determine the winner.

**Q** Who scored the most goals in a single game?

**A** Forward Joe Malone of the Quebec Bulldogs had quite a day on January 31, 1920. Malone scored seven goals in a 10–6 win over the Toronto St. Patricks. Malone's record has stood for almost 100 years. But when he initially broke it, the previous record was only three weeks old. Newsy Lalonde of the Montreal Canadiens had scored six goals against the Bulldogs on January 10, 1920.

**Q** Who is the first coach in NHL history to lose a Stanley Cup Final Game 7 with two different teams?

**A** Mike Babcock has that unfortunate honor. He led the Mighty Ducks of Anaheim to the Stanley Cup Finals in 2002–03. They lost in seven games to the New Jersey Devils. Babcock won the Cup in 2008 with the Detroit Red Wings. But the next year, Babcock and the Wings lost in the Finals to the Pittsburgh Penguins in seven games.

**Buffalo Sabres captain Brian Gionta is one of many former Boston College stars in the NHL.**

**Q** **Which US college had the most former players in the NHL in 2013–14?**

**A** Boston College had 26 former players playing in the NHL that season. The University of Wisconsin was second with 21, and the University of Michigan had 19.

Michigan State University (17) and the University of Minnesota (16) completed the top five.

**Q  Who was the first NHL player to be born in the United States?**

A Billy Burch was born in Yonkers, New York, and grew up in Toronto, Canada. Burch became the first US-born player in the NHL in 1923 when he signed with the Hamilton Tigers. He won the Hart Trophy in 1925. Burch was inducted into the Hockey Hall of Fame in 1974.

**Q  Which two players hold the all-time record for game-winning goals in the Stanley Cup Playoffs?**

A Wayne Gretzky and Brett Hull each scored 24 career game-winning goals in the Stanley Cup Playoffs. Gretzky is the NHL leader in playoff goals with 122. Hull is fourth with 103.

**Brett Hull, *left*, and Wayne Gretzky were briefly teammates in St. Louis.**

**Q** Which former defenseman holds the career record for highest plus/minus rating?

**A** Defenseman Larry Robinson spent 17 of his 20 NHL seasons with the Montreal Canadiens. The ace defenseman finished his career a plus–730. A player gets a plus-1 when he is on the ice for one of his team's even-strength goals. Players on the ice for an opponent's even-strength goal get a minus-1. That means Robinson was on the ice for 730 more even-strength goals by his team than by his opponents. Boston Bruins legend Bobby Orr, also a defenseman, is second with a plus-597.

**WHICH FOUR AWARDS DID WASHINGTON CAPITALS STAR ALEX OVECHKIN SWEEP IN THE 2007–08 SEASON?**

Ovechkin won the Maurice Richard Trophy (most goals), the Art Ross Trophy (most points), the Lester B. Pearson Award (most outstanding player as voted by NHLPA, renamed the Ted Lindsay Award in 2010), and the Hart Trophy (NHL MVP). He also led Russia to a gold medal in the World Championships and the Washington Capitals to a division title that season.

# TRIVIA QUIZ

**1** **Wayne Gretzky began his NHL career with which team?**

a. Edmonton Oilers

b. Los Angeles Kings

c. St. Louis Blues

d. New York Rangers

**2** **How many teams are in the NHL?**

a. 24

b. 28

c. 30

d. 32

**3** **Mario Lemieux wore which jersey number during his career with the Pittsburgh Penguins?**

a. 10

b. 66

c. 68

d. 99

**4** **The Calgary Flames moved from which city in 1980?**

a. Dallas

b. Atlanta

c. Kansas City

d. Denver

**5** Who was the last NHL player to play without a helmet?

a. Wayne Gretzky

b. Mark Messier

c. Craig MacTavish

d. Jaromir Jagr

**6** Along with the Mighty Ducks of Anaheim, which expansion team joined the NHL in 1993?

a. Tampa Bay Lightning

b. Minnesota Wild

c. San Jose Sharks

d. Florida Panthers

**7** Which NHL team was the last to win two consecutive Stanley Cups?

a. Montreal Canadiens

b. Detroit Red Wings

c. Pittsburgh Penguins

d. Washington Capitals

**8** Where did the Dallas Stars play before moving to Texas in 1993?

a. Minnesota

b. Michigan

c. Alaska

d. Pennsylvania

**9** Which is the only NHL team to win five consecutive Stanley Cup championships?

a. New York Rangers

b. Chicago Blackhawks

c. Detroit Red Wings

d. Montreal Canadiens

*Answers on page 47

# GLOSSARY

**assist**
A pass or a shot that leads to a teammate's goal.

**draft**
The process by which leagues determine which teams will sign new players coming into the league.

**even strength**
When both teams have the same number of skaters on the ice.

**expansion**
When a league grows by adding a new team or teams.

**hat trick**
When a player scores three goals in a game.

**overtime**
The time added to the end of a game if no winner is decided during regulation time.

**points**
Goals or assists.

**puck**
A hard, black rubber disk used in hockey.

**rookie**
A first-year player.

# FOR MORE INFORMATION

## Books

Graves, Will. *The Best Hockey Players of All Time*. Minneapolis, MN: Abdo Publishing, 2015.

Peters, Chris. *Stanley Cup Finals*. Minneapolis, MN: Abdo Publishing, 2013.

Zweig, Eric. *Super Scorers*. Richmond Hill, Ontario, Canada: Firefly Books, 2014.

## Websites

To learn more about Sports Trivia, visit **booklinks.abdopublishing.com**. These links are routinely monitored and updated to provide the most current information available.

## Answers

1. a
2. c
3. b
4. b
5. c
6. d
7. b
8. a
9. d

# INDEX

## About the Author

Dan Myers was raised in Eagan, Minnesota, and graduated with a degree in journalism from Minnesota State University. He has covered sports at all levels in the Twin Cities since 2008. He and his wife live in Hudson, Wisconsin, with their beagle, Kato.